Toddlers can Read! Guaranteed!

How to Use this Book

1. Help them Speak First: Toddlers need to say a word before they can read it. To help them speak as soon as possible, help them say the vowels before asking them to say the rest of the ABC's. Every word contains a vowel and once they learn to say "o" they can easily say "toe." When you throw all of the ABC's at once at kids, they will be confused, intimidated, and that will only slow them down.

2. See it, Say it, Read it: When possible, show a real "pan" from your kitchen, make sure kids know what "pan" is, and then ask them to say "pan." After they say it, show them how "pan" is written in this book, and ask them to read it aloud. Repeat the process a few times and then teach the next word. Eventually, they will recognize the written "pan" as you flip the pages as if you would do with flashcards.

pan

3. Obvious Pictures: Because this is the first reading book, only words that can be represent by obvious pictures are presented. For instance, the word "pan" can be represented by an obvious picture of a "pan"; but "ran" cannot be represented by an obvious picture.

4. Short Vowels Words: Because this is the first reading book, only short one-syllable words that contain short vowels are presented. The short vowels words in this book are carefully selected; they are the only short vowels words that can be represented by obvious pictures.

5. Only Letters that Sound like their Letter Name: Because this is the first reading book, a word like "cat" is avoided for now. It is avoided because "c" sounds like "k." The words presented in this book contain only letters that sound like their letter name.

6. Planned Steps: Simply follow the learning steps presented in this book. For instances, avoid teaching capital letters (**S**am), letters that do not sound like their letter name (ma**tch**), long vowels (**rai**n), blends (**str**ong), long word (pumpkin), etc. When you throw words randomly at kids, they will be confused, intimidated, and that will only slow them down.

7. Placing Words in a Queue: All the sounds we call phonics are placed in a queue awaiting their turn to be introduced one-at-a-time. For instance, "cat" is placed in a queue because it contains a hard "c." Every step in this book is carefully planned and no words are randomly thrown at kids to learn to read.

8. Guaranteed Reading and Counting: This book is for ages 1 to 3 years. Using this unique book, you are guaranteed to teach your toddlers to read 30 basic words and to count using 10 numbers.

8. Cumulative Books: The next reading & math book your child will need is *Reading & Math for Preschool*, which is for ages 3 to 4 years. The book *Reading & Math for Kindergarten* is for ages 4 to 5 years. The book *Reading & Math for First Grade* is for age 6.

9. Reading Achieved before Going to School: Using these reading & math books, you can easily teach your children to read before sending them to school. You will then enable first-grade teachers to teach other subjects instead.

10. *Read Instantly*: Most of the reading material in these books is taken from the book *Read Instantly*, which is a book to teach phonics to all ages.

11. Math Lessons for Toddles: The last ten pages in this book are to help toddlers say the number, recognize the written number, and then count the number of dogs on each page. For instance, kids first learn to say **ten** and then they see the written number **10** next to ten dogs. After that, they learn to count the number of dogs on that page, which are 10 dogs. If there are ten dogs on a page, the number 10 is written on that page.

About the Author

Linguist Camilia Sadik is the author of ten other books to teach phonics and spelling to children and adults. The titles of the books are *Read Instantly*, *Learn to Spell 500 Words a Day* (six volumes: A, E, I, O, U, Consonants), *100 Spelling Rules*, *The Compound Words* (7,000 Compound & Hyphenated Words) and *How to Teach Phonics - Teachers' Guide*.

SpellingRules.com

Visit SellingRules.com to learn about all the phonics and spelling books by Linguist Camilia Sadik.

Copyrights 2014

5

fan

pan

rat

hat

van

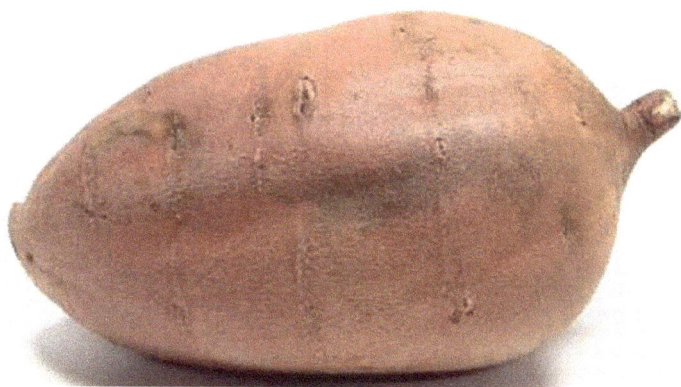

yam

ĕ

bed

pen

hen

10

ten

jet

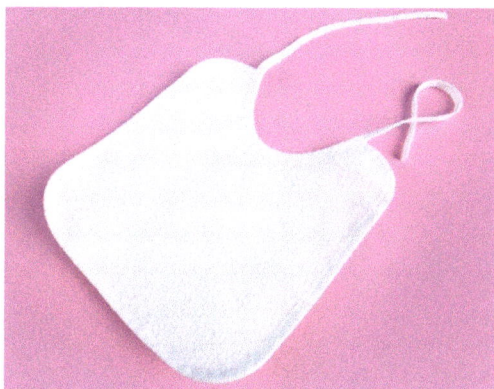

bib

6

six

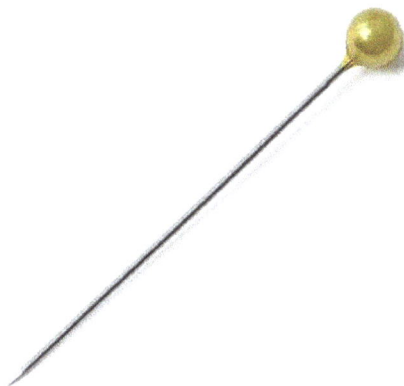

pin

fin

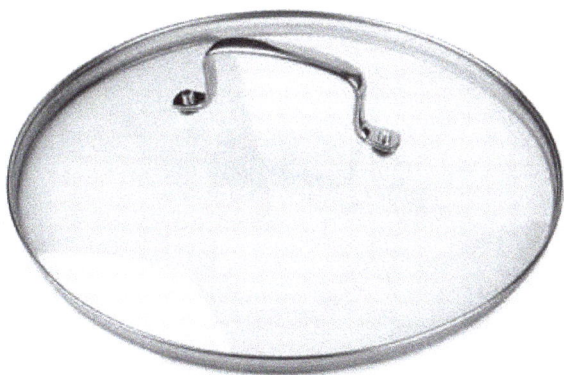

lid

pot

box

fox

mop

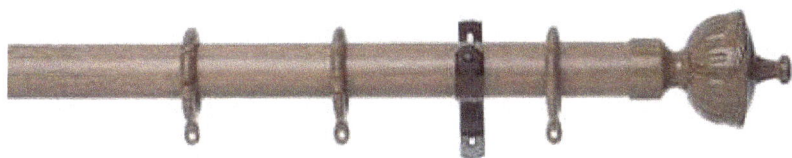

rod

pup

tub

bus

sun

bun

nut

hut

mud

bud

Math for Toddlers

Help toddlers say and then recognize the following numbers. After they can say and then recognize the numbers, help them count the number of dogs on each page:

1

3

4

5

6

7

8

9

10